Copyright © 2025 by Educate Learners

Published by Educate Learners

All rights reserved. No part of this publication may be reproduced, distributed, or transmitted in any form or by any means, including photocopying, recording, or other electronic or mechanical methods, without the prior written permission of the publisher, except in the case of brief quotations embodied in critical reviews and certain other noncommercial uses permitted by copyright law.

First Printing, 2025.

ISBN: 978-1-951573-59-1

www.educatelearners.com

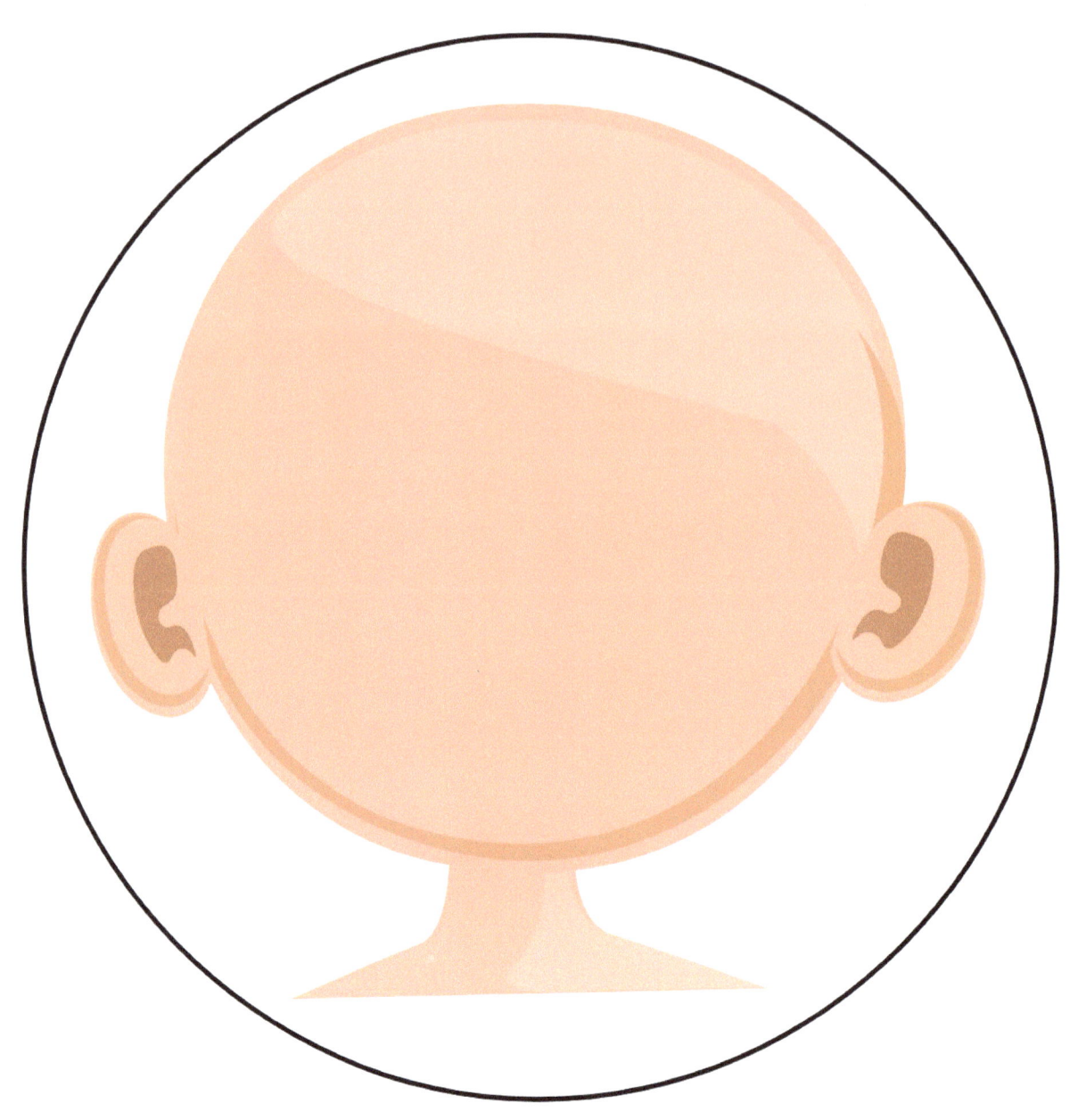

Head

Our head keeps our eyes, nose, mouth, ears and brain in one place.

Eyes

Our eyes help us see and read.

Nose

Our nose helps us breathe and smell.

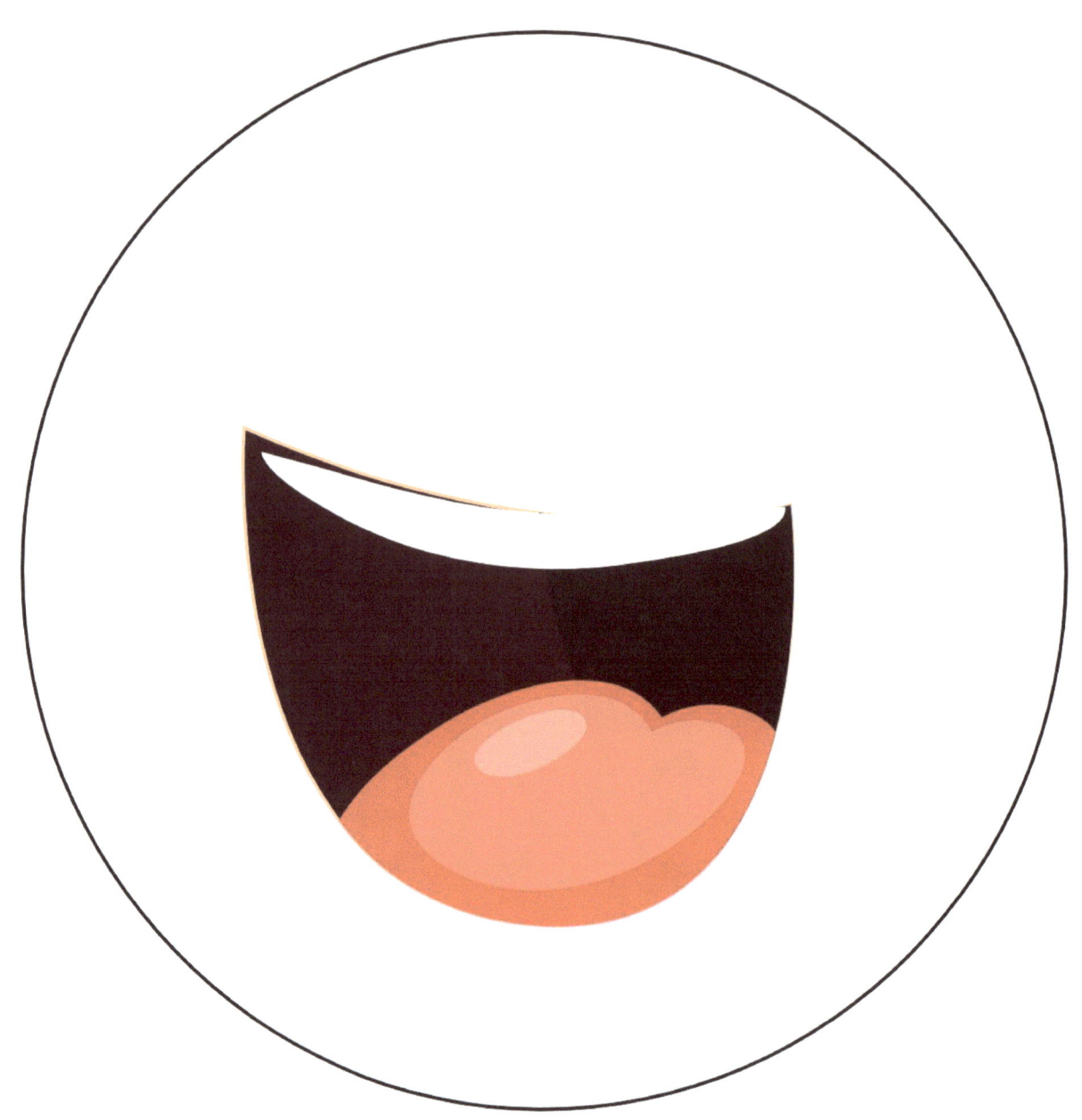

Mouth

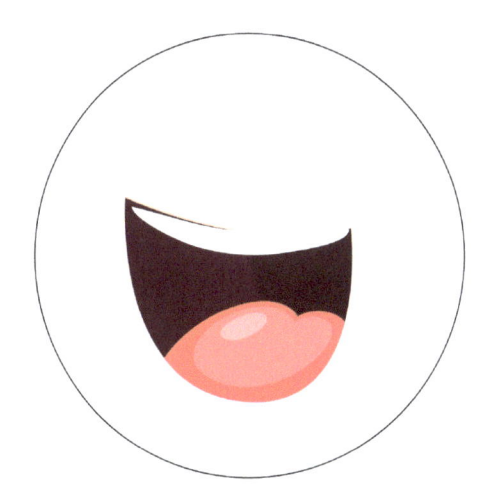

Our mouth helps us talk and smile.

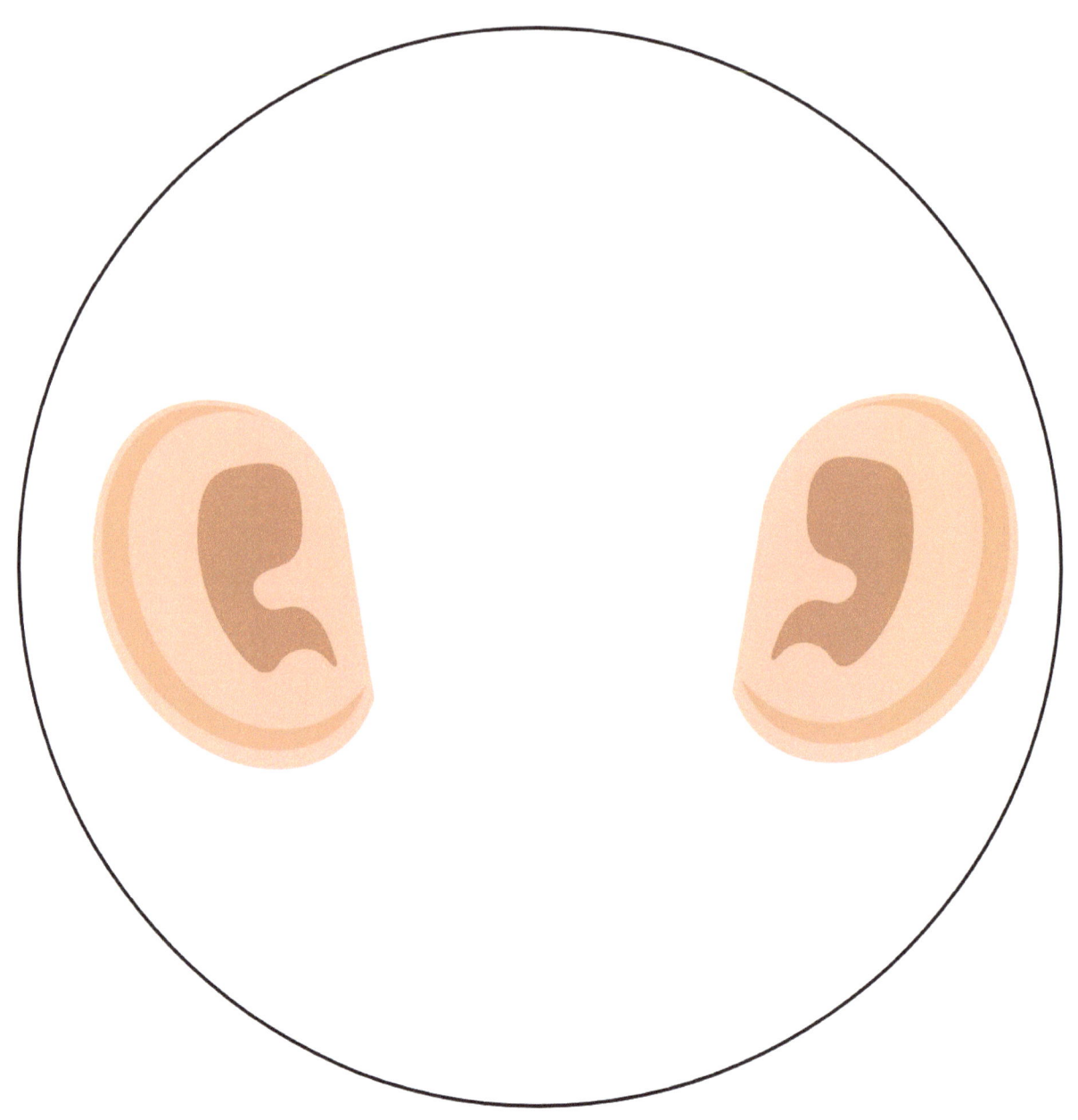

Ears

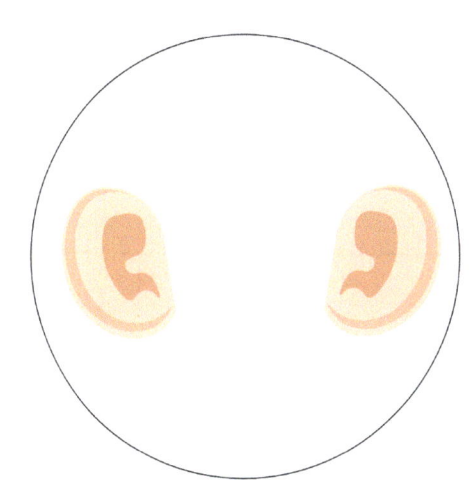

Our ears help us hear and listen.

Hair

Our hair helps keep our head warm and safe. It is also fun to style.

Eyebrows

Our eyebrows keep liquid away from our eyes and helps us express ourselves.

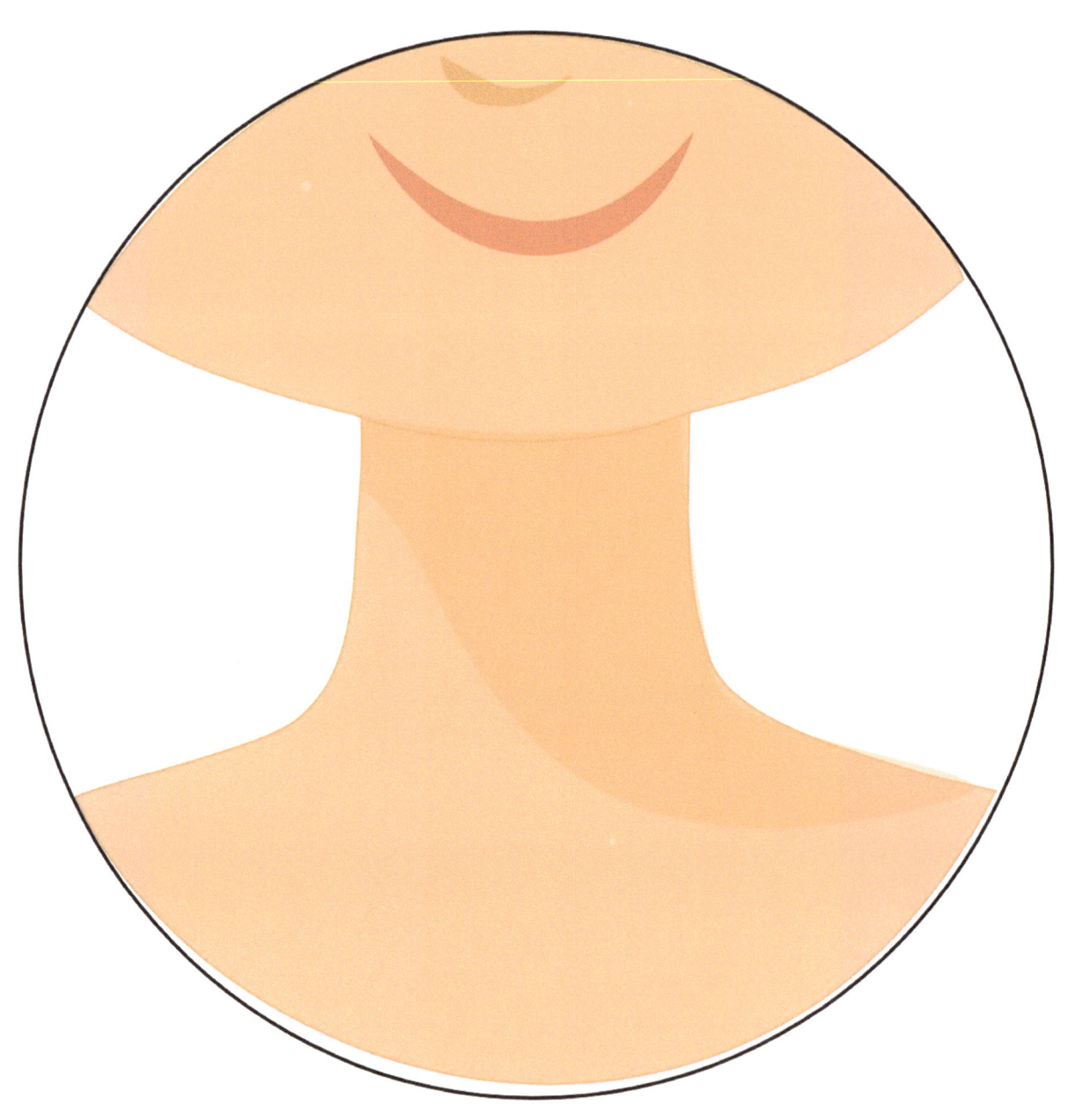

Neck

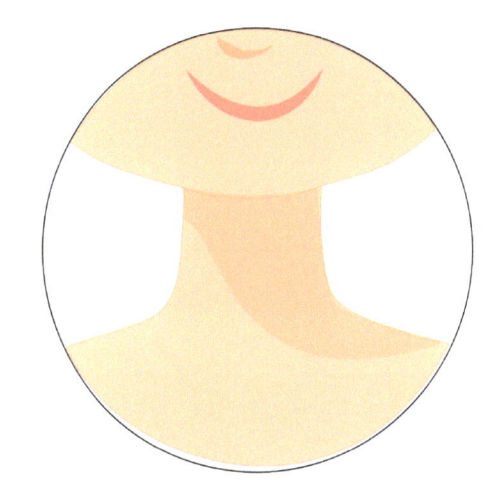

Our neck supports our head and connects it to our the rest of our body.

Teeth

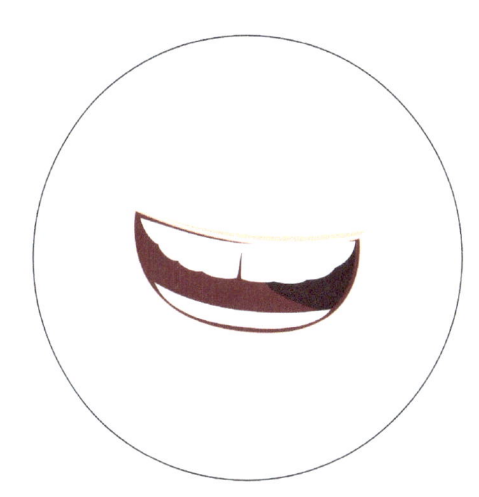

Our teeth help us to chew our food.

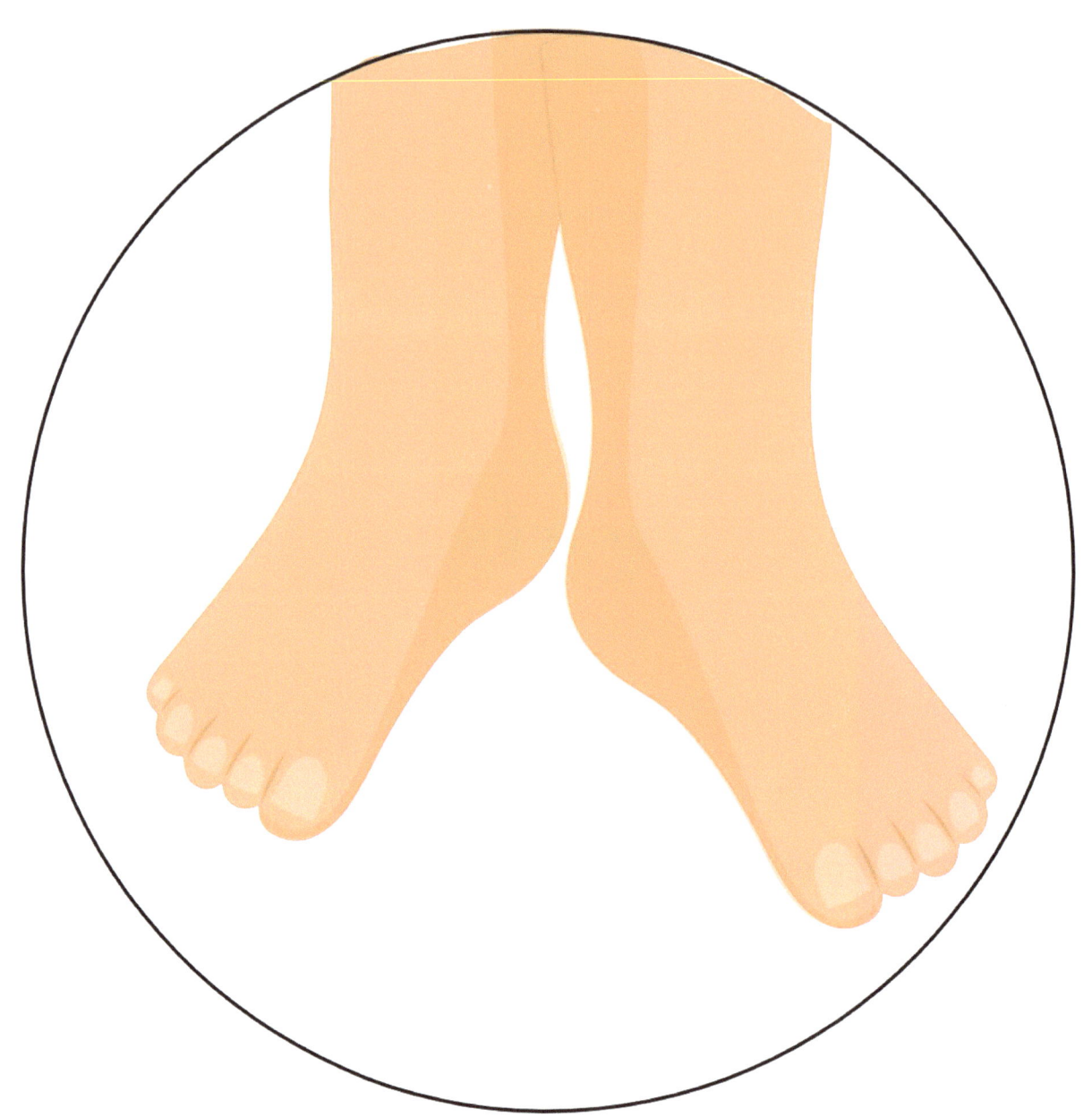

Feet

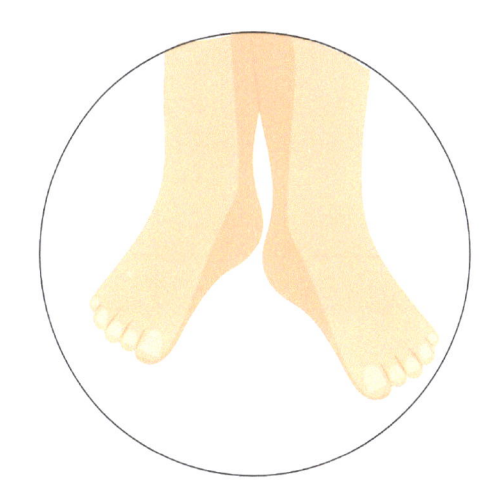

Our feet help us walk and keep our balance.

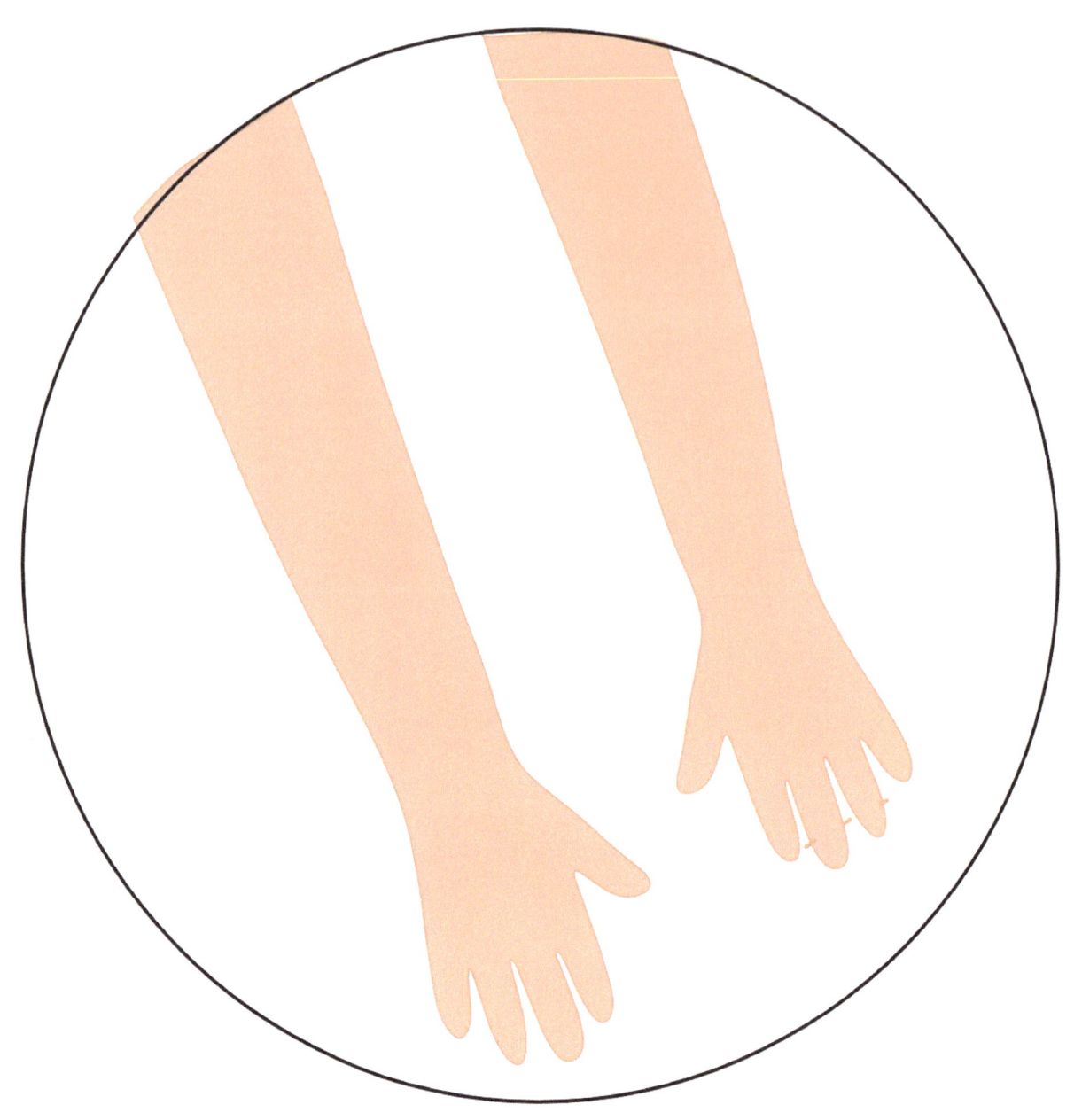

Arms

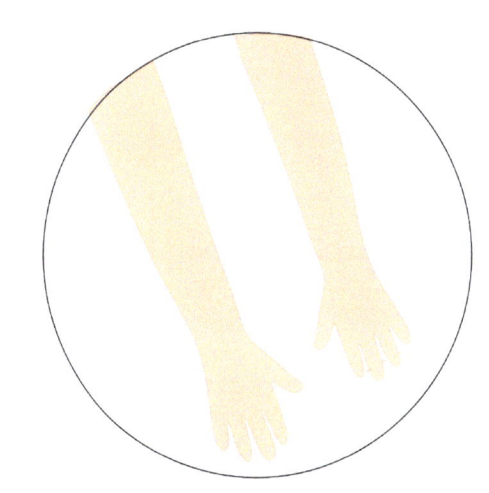

Our arms help us reach for and carry items.

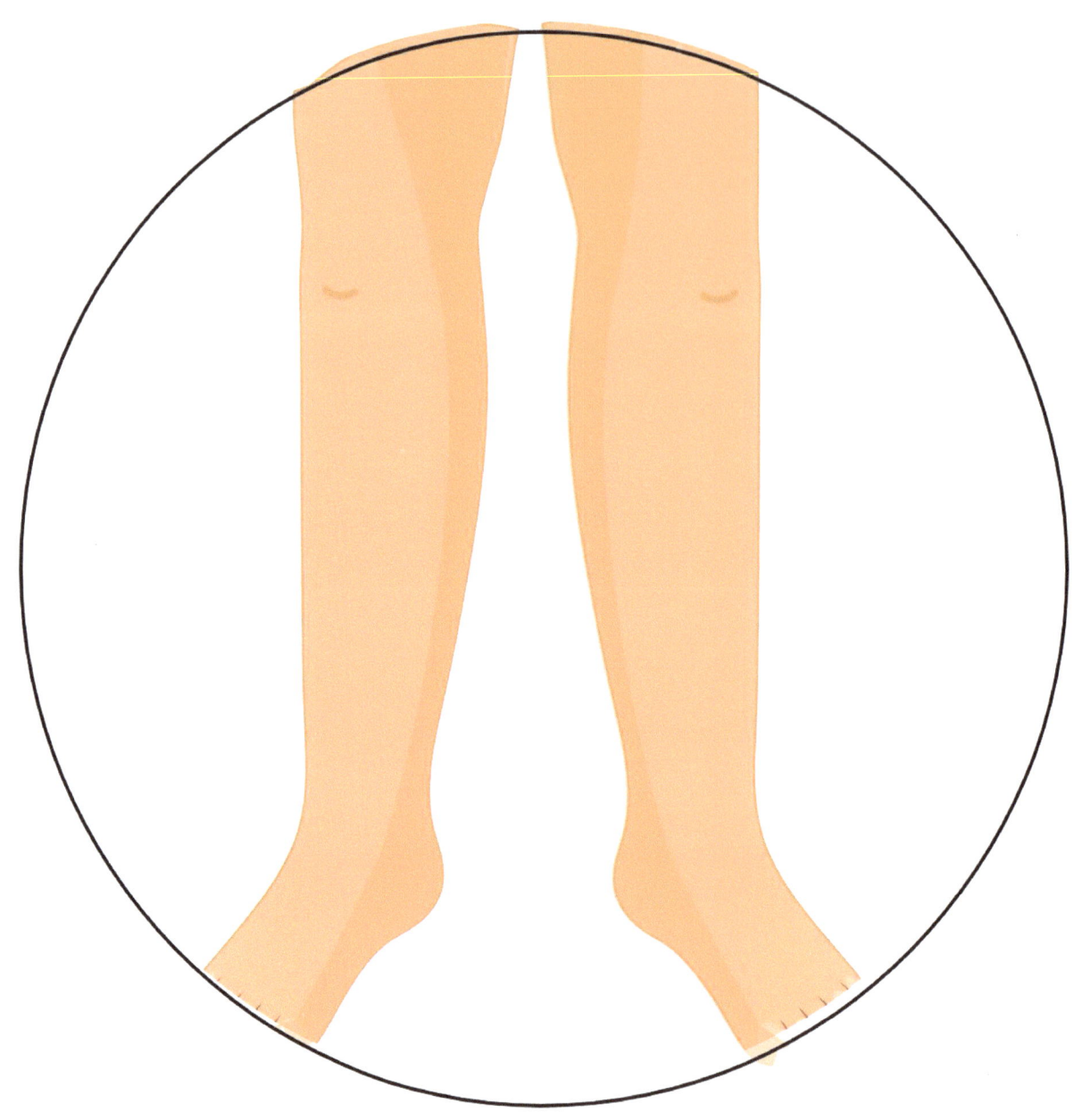

Legs

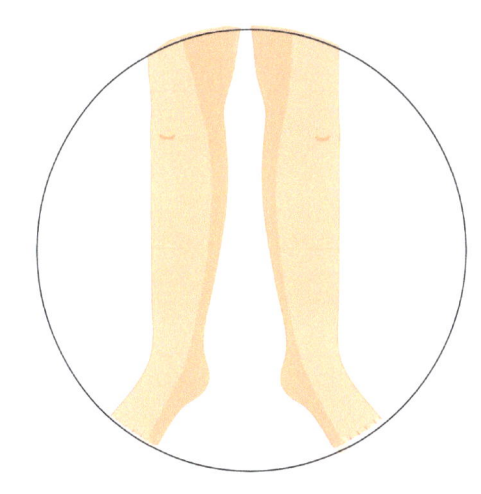

Our legs help us stand and walk.

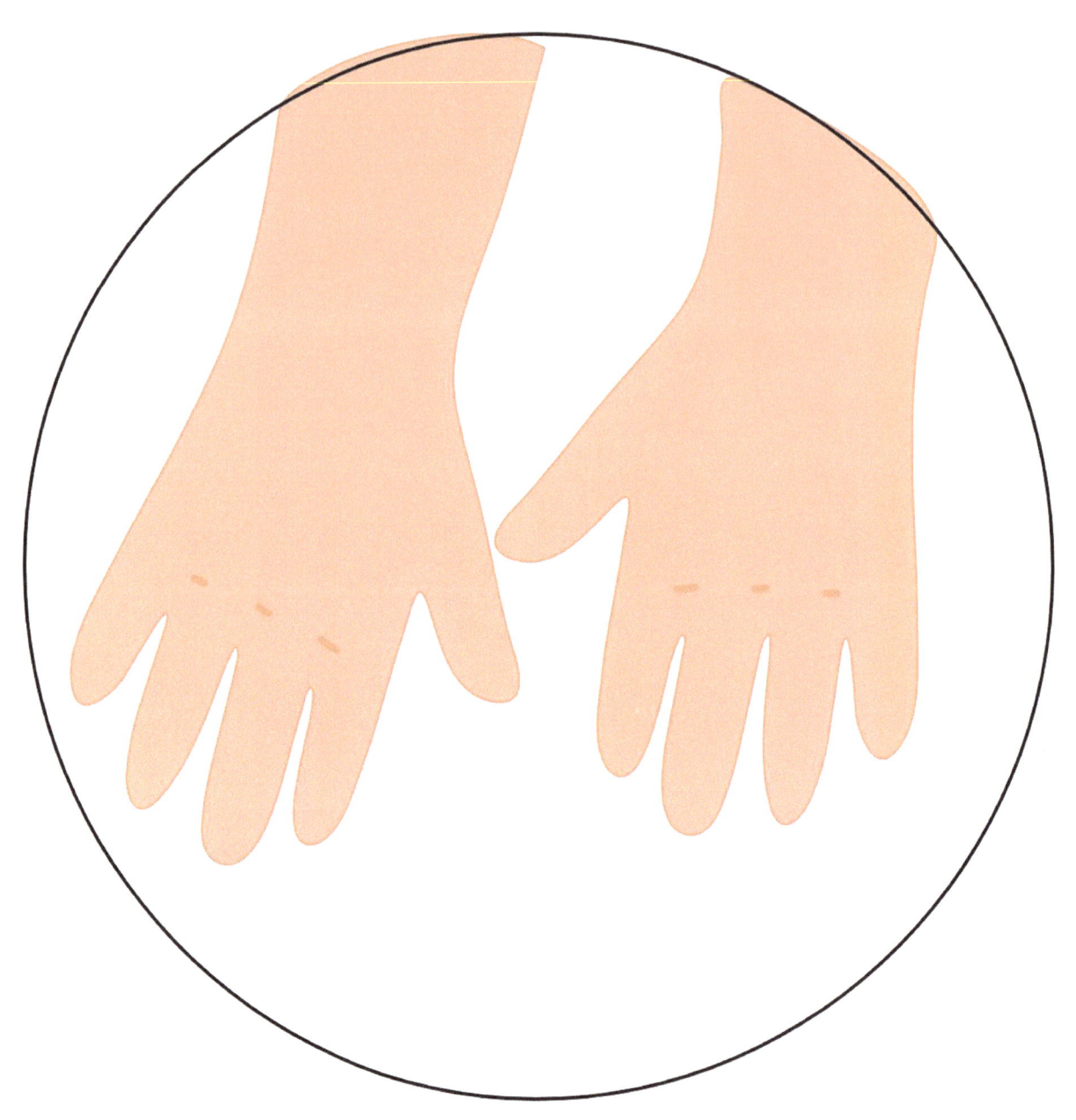

Hands

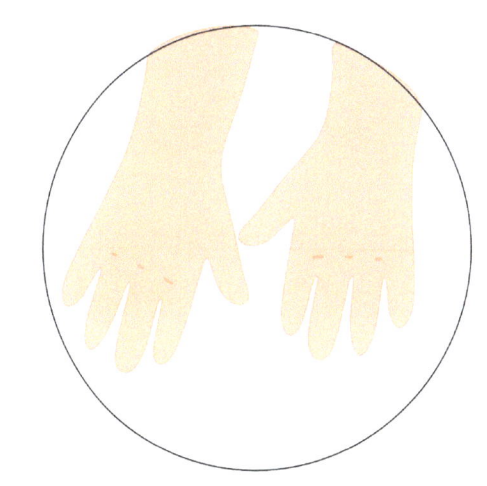

Our hands help us hold and use items to do things such as write, color or throw.

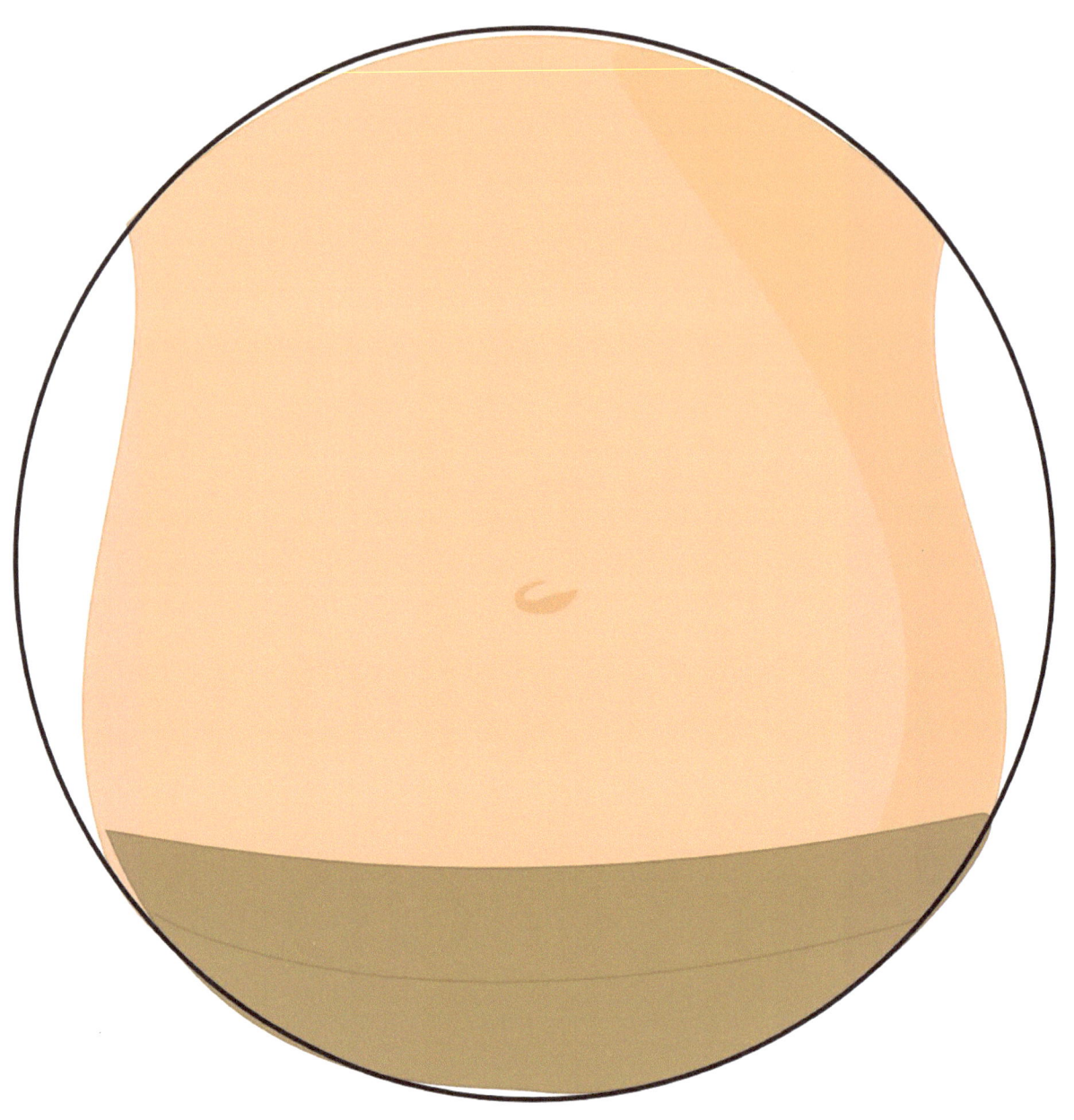

Stomach

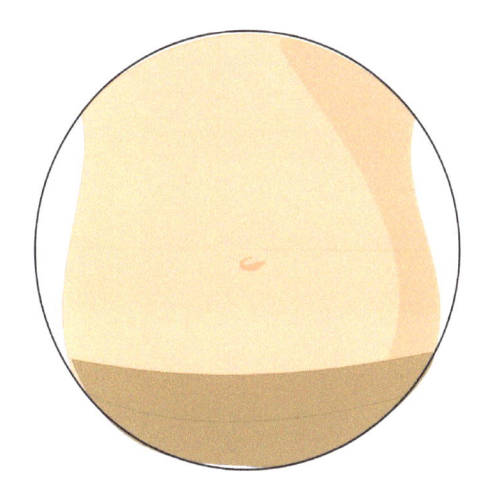

Our stomach is where our food goes after we eat.

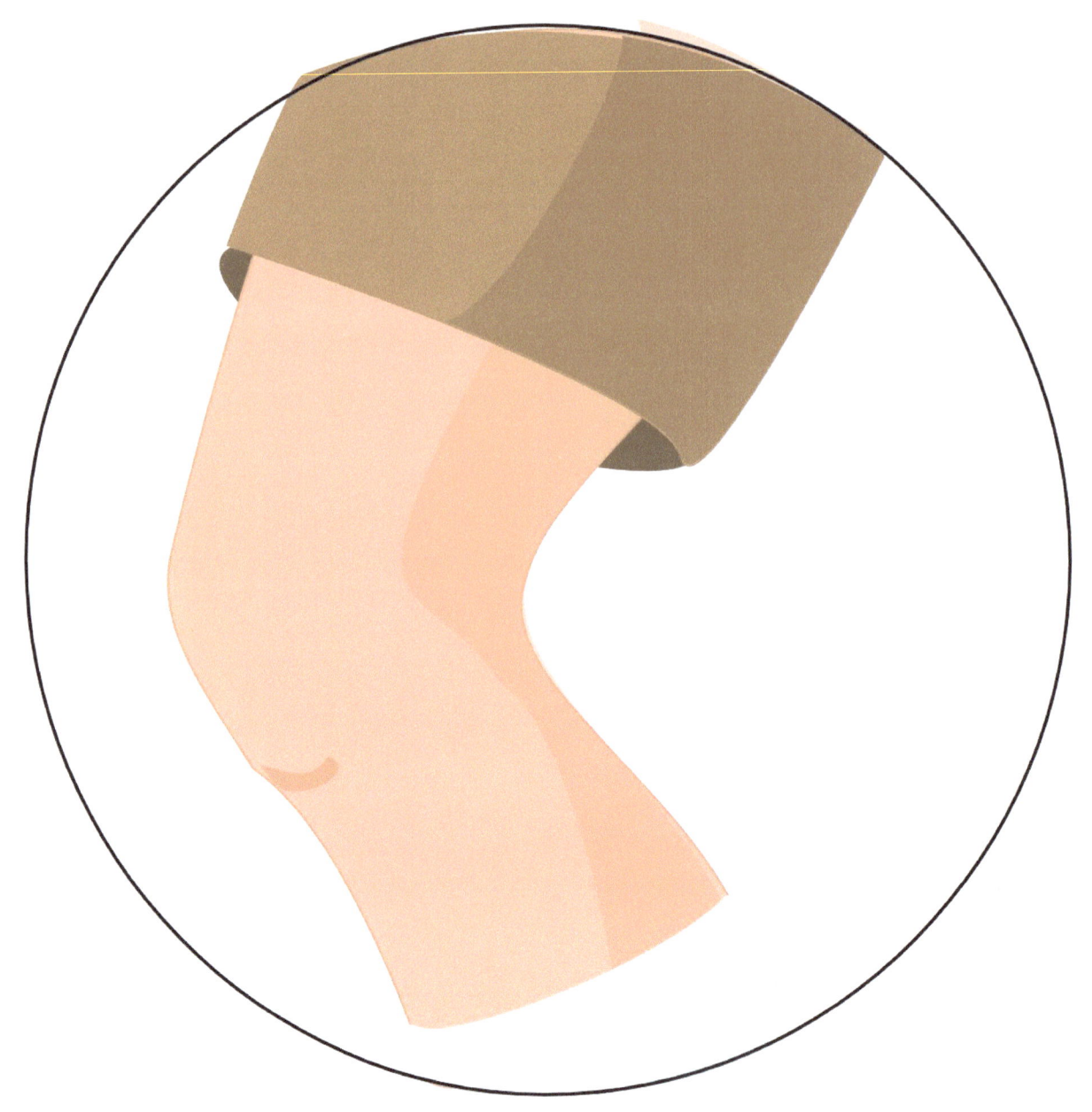

Knee

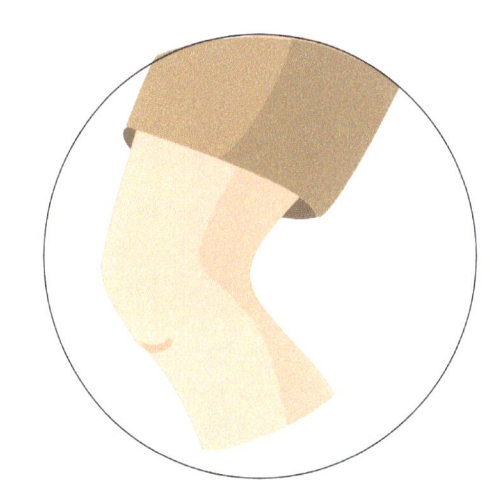

Our knees help us bend and jump.

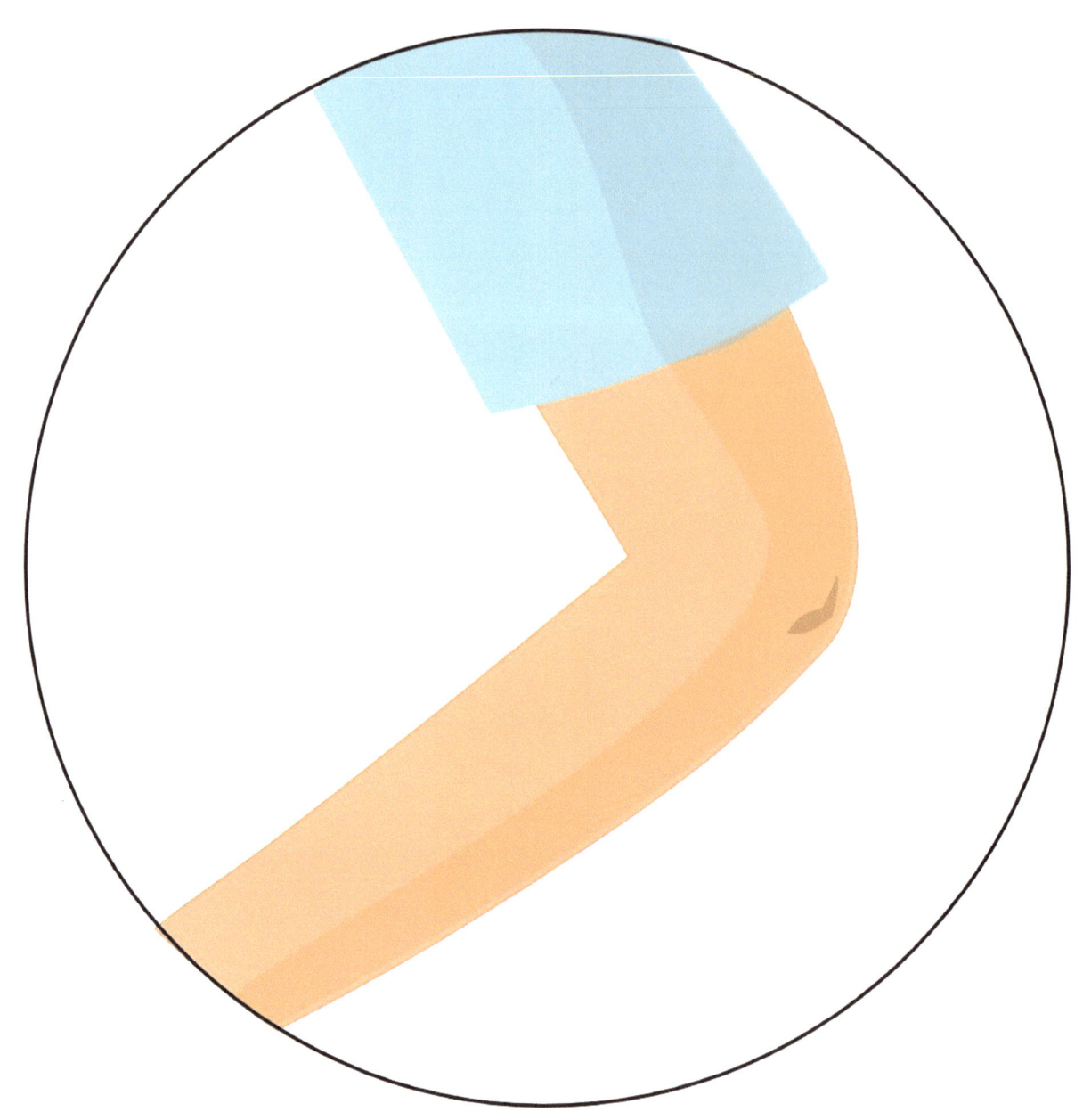

Elbow

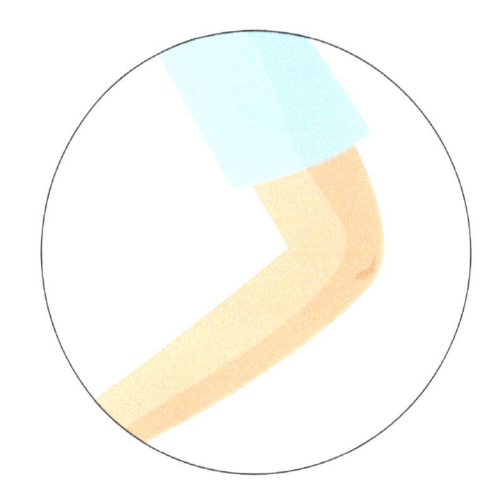

Our elbows help us bend our arms and pick up items.

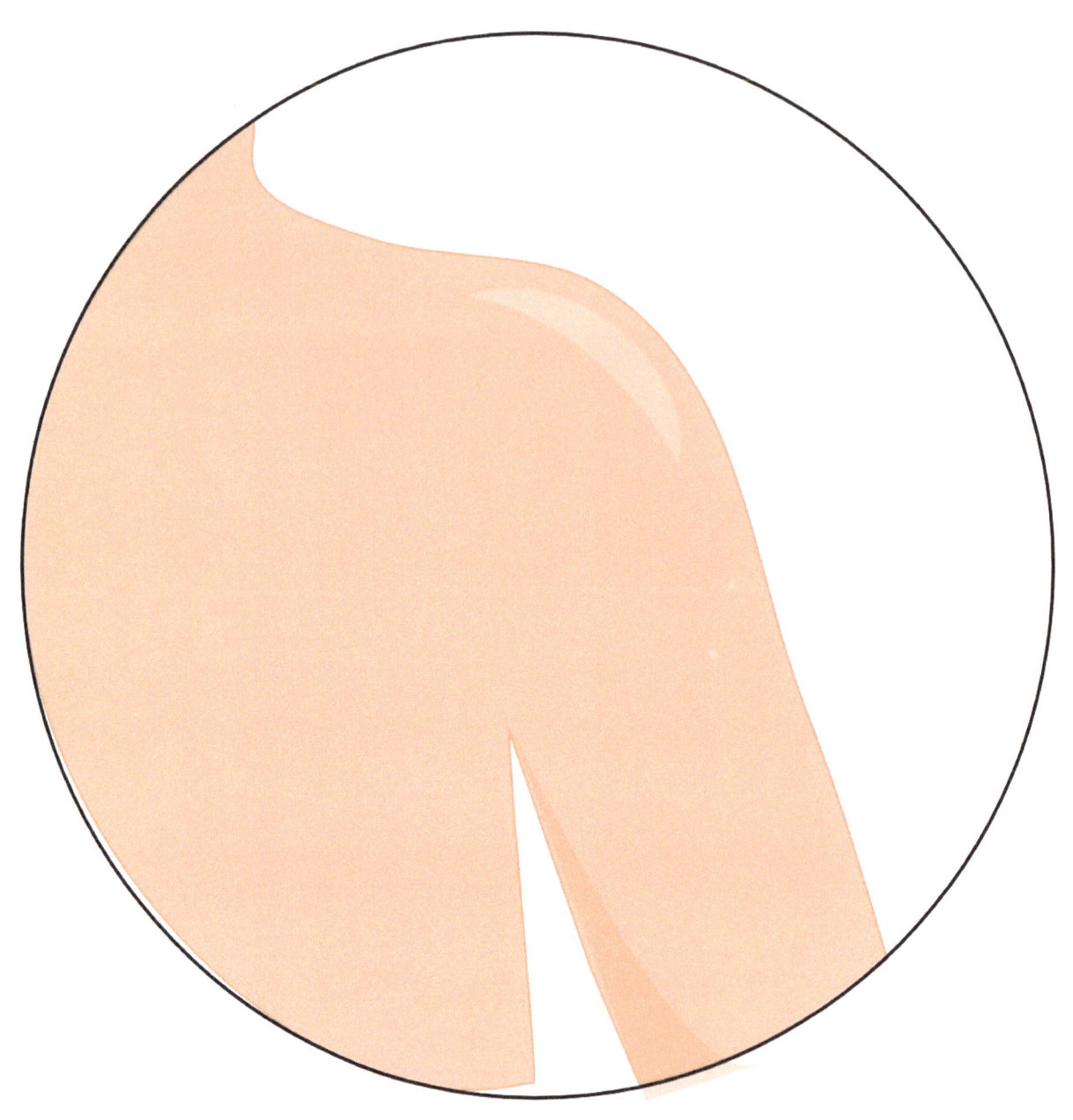

Shoulder

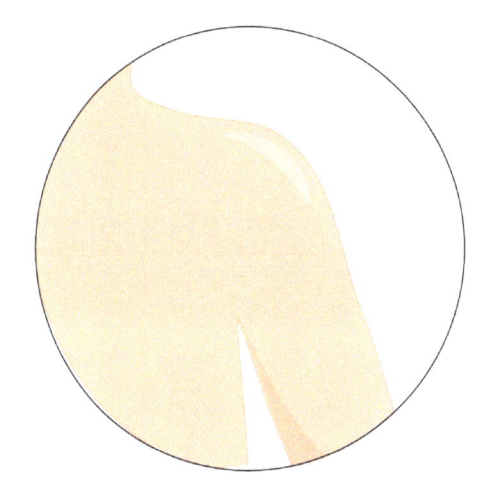

Our shoulders help our arms move and connects them to our body.

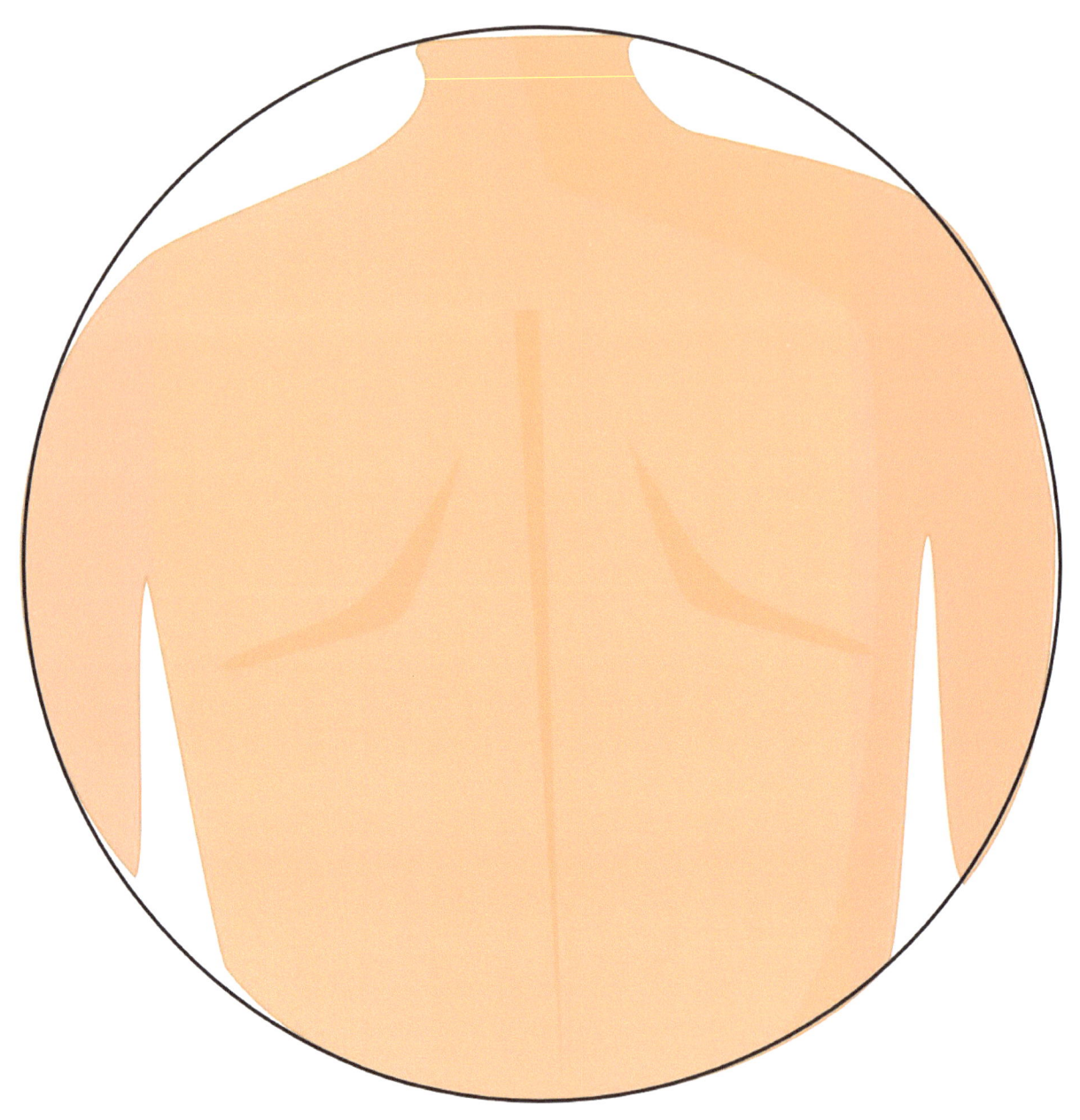

Back

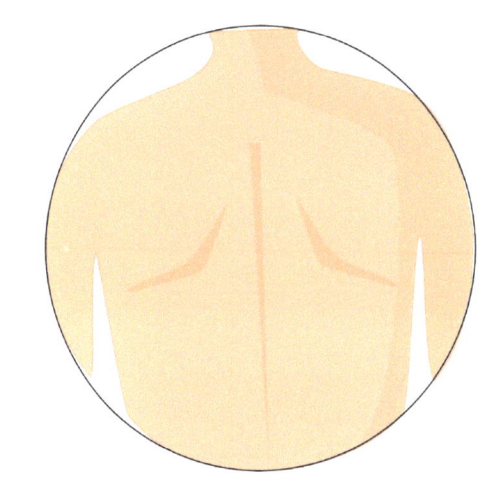

Our back supports our body and protects our spine.

Thank you for reading!

Get a free year long subscription to our online education resource library when you purchase any one of our books.

Code: EDBOOKS

educatelearners.com

www.ingramcontent.com/pod-product-compliance
Lightning Source LLC
Chambersburg PA
CBHW041602070526
44586CB00003BA/53